WILD CATS!

Written by Diane Muldrow
Illustrated by Greg Harris

D0113255

Copyright © 1998 McClanahan Book Company, Inc.
All rights reserved.
Published by McClanahan Book Company, Inc.
23 West 26th Street, New York, NY 10010
Printed in the U.S.A.
ISBN: 0-7681-0095-x
Reviewed by Dr. Edward M. Spevak,
Assistant Curator of Mammals at the Bronx Zoo.

Have you ever seen a cat go after a toy mouse, or try to catch a bird?

With their good eyesight and hearing—and sharp teeth and claws—house cats are a lot like their relatives, the big cats.

And big cats often look like giant house cats when they take a nap under a tree, or roll in the grass!

LION

The lion is often called the king of the beasts. It has a beautiful mane of golden hair, huge teeth, and . . . a very loud roar!

The lion grows up to 10 feet (3 meters) long. It weighs as much as 500 pounds (229 kg). Its queen, the lioness, weighs 300 pounds (137 kg). That's a lot more than most grown men weigh!

Lions are the only cats that live in family groups, called **prides**. It is the male lion's job to keep the pride safe.

FACT

Homeland: Africa; Gir Forest, NW India

Remember: It is the only cat that lives in groups!

Lions hunt as a group. That way, they're able to kill animals larger than themselves—such as wildebeests, or even young elephants or giraffes.

They can charge their prey at 40-50 miles (64.5 to 81 km) per hour. That's as fast as a car moving on a highway! Even though females do most of the hunting, the males get to eat first.

Lionesses give birth to as many as five or six babies, called **cubs**. The cubs stay close to their mother for up to two years.

Lion cubs spend lots of time chasing and pouncing on each other. This is how they learn to defend themselves and hunt. Once they're grown, males leave their sisters and mother behind to form their own pride.

TIGER

What's larger, heavier, and more ferocious than a lion? A tiger—it is the biggest cat of all!

The male Siberian tiger weighs over 600 pounds (275 kg). It can grow to be 14 feet long (4 meters), nose to tail. That is twice as long as your living-room sofa!

Tigers live on the continent of Asia. They live in steamy hot places. And they live in very cold places, where their coats are extra thick to keep them warm.

 **FACT**

Homeland: Asia

Remember: It is the largest cat!

Tigers usually live by themselves. Their stripes help hide them in long grasses and dark forests. Each tiger has its own special stripe pattern.

Tigers eat water buffalo, cattle, and antelope. But if they're not lucky enough to catch a big animal, they'll settle for a frog! Tigers are good swimmers. They often wait for their prey near a waterhole.

LEOPARD

The leopard is the smallest of the big cats. It weighs about 100 pounds (46 kg). If you ever go to leopard country, look up in the trees! You might see a leopard in one. Leopards are very good climbers.

 **FACT**

Homeland: Southern Asia, Africa

Remember: It is the smallest big cat!

This mother leopard is carrying her cub by the loose skin of its neck. Don't worry—it doesn't hurt the cub at all!

The **"black panther"** is actually a **leopard**. It is born with black spots on a black background.

Unlike the other big cats, leopards don't usually roar—the sound they make is more of a raspy call.

SNOW LEOPARD

The snow leopard has a woolly whitish-gray coat that blends in with the snow. Its long tail comes in handy as a thick scarf! The snow leopard has always been hunted for its fur. It is very endangered today.

Snow leopards can grow to be seven feet (2 meters) long, from head to fluffy tail. They're excellent jumpers. They hunt goats, ground squirrels, antelopes, and even cattle!

FACT

Homeland: Central Asia

Remember: It loves the cold!

CLOUDED LEOPARD

The clouded leopard is not a true big cat, because it doesn't roar. It purrs!

But like big cats, it does have very long teeth. And like its distant relative the true leopard, it also climbs trees.

FACT

Homeland: Southeast Asia

Remember: It purrs!

CHEETAH

The cheetah is the "sports car" of cats. When a cheetah hunts, it moves in for the kill in a burst of speed. In only two seconds, it goes from 0 to 45 miles (0 to 72.5 km) per hour. In a few seconds, it speeds up to 70 miles (113 km) per hour! But it can only run that fast for a short time.

The cheetah has a slim, doglike body. Its flexible spine works like a spring to shoot the cheetah forward. Powerful back legs, large lungs, and extra-long claws help make the cheetah the fastest land animal in the world.

 **FACT**
Homeland: Africa

Remember: It is the fastest land animal in the world!

JAGUAR

The jaguar is a strong cat with short, sturdy legs. Males may grow as large as eight feet (2.5 meters) long. The jaguar is a good leaper and pouncer—especially when it's hungry! It likes to hunt sloths and tapirs. Since it's a good swimmer, it catches turtles and fish, too.

Jaguars don't roar very much. They tend to grunt, cough, and growl instead!

 **FACT**

Homeland: South America

Remember: It is the largest South American cat!

Which big cat is your favorite?